AFTERGLOW OF A SILVER DREAM

DEBAHUTI BORAH

ISBN 979-888606007-2

I would wholeheartedly dedicate this book to a special person in my life that I share a deep, soulful connection with. Your aura whispers of the colour silver. Thank you, for helping me see the world as I see today. Thank you, for being the inspiration behind this book.

Contents

Contents

Preface

On a cold, winter evening, sitting alone in retrospection, I decided to write a poem titled "Silver"—and that was the beginning of a romance that led to this book. Love comes in mystical ways in one's life, and my life is ordinarily beautiful in experiencing the romance of a lifetime set in twenty-five days. These twenty-five days, I wrote a poem each day as I traced my mind and what the heart had to speak in volumes, marking the venture of this book so close to my soul.

With this brief history, I leave the poems in the hands of my readers—to treat them as a voice to the love that they feel, never lost, even if you cannot be with that person.

1. Silver

Silver linings that you talk about
Heavy with love,
I felt a bit, then I felt more,
So heavy with love.
I am melting in this teardrop
When you talk about melting leaves
Under drops of a crying waterfall.
You cannot choose between two,
And I respect it so,
And I respect it so,
For I have fallen
Under the silver moon
With melancholia playing in waves
As our eyes meet in intense fires.
Come, feel me again,
With the world of you
Bringing an eternity
Of aching bond
Which I lost before I met your
Fast-beating heart
Snuggled in your chest
Through dizzying city lights.
You were silver

I was gold;
No! It isn't a confusion
But a plea to the universe
To let us live
One moment, after another,
In an embrace of a lost cloud
Holding a glimmer
Of silver linings.

2. Cusp

I have been wrong,
If you would like to see
Where my eyes would sink
To a disastrous abyss;
I would keep on loving
You forever,
For I have never been
So right too
About four hands
In a cusp between
Two sunsigns,
Two penny worth
Of beating hearts
Dreaming of millions
Of loving under the stars alone.
Episodes after another
Rush in
For your hands would be
Intact with another
For a binding
Of a lifetime,
As I would heal my way
Through dense tears

Of loving grief
That I choose,
To be wrong
If I be right.

3. Mercy

Skin-deep in mercy
I scale the heights
Of your terrain
Where you dreams
Of making love
To your lover
Under the stars
Nestled above the mountains.
I dream a dream too,
Of us,
In a safe embrace
That sets us free.
Dreams, I have seen many,
Of us this morning;
I am seeing one now,
Of grave positions
In life,
Of succumbing
To social constructs
Heading with a people-pleaser
For all we know its worth
And our own,
And of us.

4. Thirsty

Blood-thirsty moon
That we saw from the rooftop
That evening of blissful tears
Turned silver later,
Reflecting the scars
That you hold
In turbulence within.
It changed colours
From the first time
You looked into my eyes,
As I spoke of lovers past,
To the time our lips met
In soul-thirsty valleys
Of our souls,
Trailing a dream of camping
Somewhere in the mountains
Under a song of
wicked games.
The gimmick lies
In anticipated worth
Of social frenzy
Sitting on my Moon,
Devouring the silver

Back to emotion-thirsty loom.

5. What Is It That We Have?

You ask me,
"What is it that we have?"
I answer,
"Speak to me with your eyes,
Where your soul sings
Right through,
Drowning in chaotic haze,
Yet rising—slowly,
To be a bird with silver wings.
Speak to me,
As you draw me closer,
And we breathe
Under the same breath,
In proximity we bathe
In lives living.
Speak to me,
With your fingertips
As they dance with mine,
Twinkling auras
Of the stars beyond.
Speak to me, softly,
Of the love we share,

And keep everything else
A secret
To be maintained
By the universe of us."

6. Void Goodbyes

We only said goodbyes
Void of meanings
In them.
I yearn and I yearn
And I know
You do too,
For you tell me,
What of goodbyes
Mean nothing of them.
I long and I long
And I know
You do too,
For you tell me,
What of love we shared
Meant all of it.

7. Fly Away

Tell me what you are thinking
Now
About flying away
With me.
We find a home
In the coastline
And make tender steps
Upon it
To awaken the senses
That have hibernated
Through summers and winters
Of forgone feelings.
You are parking
An aura in my field
Of grass filled with dew-drops,
As a pup plays over it
In wanton playfulness.
I set you free;
All I want is you
To be liberated in love.
I set you free, you tell me.
You set me free, I tell you.
We walk the horizon

Rising above the chains
That tie us
To worldly worldliness
As we explore the universe
In a lifetime of a week,
Or less.
Let's fly away,
Only to return healed
To face the cages
That shall consume
Our souls of free-will.
Let's live for once,
Let's fly away.

8. Let Go

I wait for you patiently,
So that we may call it too close
To have what we have,
Because we are scared
Of forest fires under rain
Smoking of burnt ashes
Without trays,
Intensifying the fires within
That engulf us
To a ball of energy
Unable to contain.
And society fears that;
So we must let go.
So we must let go.

9. Decisions

I don't know why
The clocks stop ticking
On my wrist
Carrying lines
Of evaporated torture.
I must make a decision,
And quick –
A quicksand of moments
Like we hurried kisses
In lanes drawn by
What would not be accepted.
Clocks are ticking,
Just not in my blood.
Time stands in front of me,
Scaring to flap its huge wings away,
And I solemnly accept
What it has to say
In an effort to stay calm.
In an effort to stay sane.
In an effort to stay, still.
In an effort not to stay still.
I love with fervent ardour,
For this clock is ticking,

And it is only a one-sided street
Without branches,
For you have let fate decide you
And the glimmer in your wristwatch
As much as that in my eyes,
As I wait on decisions
To see you leave.

10. Happy Blankets

Let my body slide under
The blanket, so cozy,
So heavy, leaving me
In·warmth of an embrace.
Tumultuous thoughts of
"What I am supposed to do?"
Fondle my chest
As I draw your face closer to it,
Leaving all my worries
For another month
After next year.
It's not a relief
That my blanket has creases
Of bloody haunts,
Daunting tales of washers
Being waved by human-made floods
Upon valleys so deep
In thick secrets, swelling.
I rest my eyes
To meet your lips
Another time
Under a blanket of stars
As happiness seeps in

Like a cosmos uniting
In vision of an afterglow,
Taking mercy of no one,
But treading, treading
Into our souls.

11. Romance

Romance is just a word
That I stutter
In your marmalade presence.
Following my sins
Of towering horizons,
Gelling with the clouds,
Reflecting clouds incredibly green.
Lying to myself,
I lie on you,
Telling myself I would be okay
When you have to dress up
And leave.
For now, I soak in
The warmth of your veins
Tangled with mine,
Meaning life or death
At no cost,
Because it's only living from hereon,
In separation,
With romance of a lifetime.

12. Boisterous Heart

Boisterous heart,
Would you pay heed?
You drag me down marshlands
And tell me it's only plain
Living in plains.
Plans of setting fire
To our souls
Had entered your scheme
The day we met, bounded.
I let go
Of what I had,
But you played strings
On drums,
Beating your pace higher.
A dog carelessly crossed the road,
And you took after
To be a pup
Running amidst wheeling roads.
Boisterous heart,
Pay heed.
It's not in my hands
To bind you too,
Like he is bound

To his.

13. Open Windows

Open windows in my room,
Like my heart for you,
Seek love in undisguised forms
Of lullabies for the setting sun.
The orange light only lingered
Like your fingers
Over my cold-blooded flesh,
Mantling a cushion of freshness
Seeping in like fog
On a winter evening.
Come right back,
Before I shut it (shut it!)
Tight, for tonight.
I am left in longing
For an ephemeral moment
Of getaway, like wild hearts
Swaying, swaying in the winds
Of my cold room.
Open windows
For the evening,
I seek you in my senses
As the fog turns wild,
And I shut it (shut it!)

Tight, for tonight.

14. Freefalling

Daunting face of death
Doesn't scare me
As much as it scares me
To lose myself
Among faceless straws
Of beckoning darkness.
Let me say
I stepped into fearless,
Meeting you at a standstill
Of haunting hills
And debating heartbeats.
You brought me closer
To my soul to see
The light I was carrying
To free myself
And others
Of haunting branches
Upon a gravy tree.
Death doesn't scare me
Anymore;
But I fear, I fear
Losing myself of myself

15. For the Kill

Kill me with a vine.
Kill me with two.
Thunder only resounds
When a deed has done wound.
You speak
About a black and white rainbow
Bringing rain with no meaning.
And I stand under it
To find my pot of luck,
Running towards peaks
Of desolate wants.
If you don't love me now,
I have a heart of two
To love us anew.
Hush about the rainbows you see
In your favourite colours,
For the world calls us crazy
(Which we are)
And drags us out of it.
But you are in tolerance of
What I am not.
You are in need of something
I will never be.

Kill me with three vines,
And I will still survive
With my head under water
And soul over the clouds.

16. Social Abyss

Don't you say, my Darling,
That you hate yourself.
The world doesn't hold you
With love,
And that's not on you
To feel obliged.
To feel worthless.
Worthless is society
To push you through denting teeth
With a chatter of the knives,
For making you feel the misery
Of letting go of your lover's hand
To hold another
For some reason
That I cannot fathom
Even in the abyss I have called my own.

17. Aisles

Oh, look! How different we look.
How differently we look.
You look forward
To walking down the aisle
With a hand in yours
Forever,
While I look forward
To walk down one
And take a seat
To fly.
Yours is a lifetime,
Mine's a lifetime crumpled in two days.
Yours is to see the world with her,
Mine's to meet the seas with you.
Tell me, if one's not happy,
What's the aisle of Death worth?

18. Misty Stories

Who is going to say what we shared
If not for these raindrops
That envelop us to kiss our cheeks
On this misty evening?
They swirl and dance around us
In the form of a thick blanket
With sane intentions to keep us warm,
Only chilling us further.
Maybe they had a plan,
Maybe they didn't,
But we cuddled to keep warm.
And maybe that's what
They would speak about
When they dissolve into
Stories of their own belonging.

19. The Road Taken

The road is our song.
Let's sing along the way
In jolly heartbeats
Fastened to seatbelts.
We dreamt of a horizon
We are nearly reaching,
Ditching seashells speaking
Of unnerving plans.
We mount a canopy
As we rise
To succumb to our feelings
Yet again,
In a comfortable place
We would call our home for a day
Or two.
The consolidation speaks
In volumes of isolation
Yet to arrive at the juncture.
For now I bid adieu
To the kaleidoscopic way
And live a wildflower
For another day.

20. A Secret Song

"Life is a note of misery
Played in a beautiful song,"
He said,
Looking straight into my eyes
As the stars blinked back
At the sight of us
Like I said,
"Heavy with love."
I died a thousand times
And lived again,
To play the beautiful song
That he so earnestly talked about.
We sat under the naked sky,
Naked in emotions
Of belonging to one another,
Just for a little while
That we have left.
And no wonder life is a trek
Down to a beautiful sky,
And up to a scenic waterfall,
To feel the kiss
Of my euphoria gushing out
While you make love to me,

Under a tired ceiling
That has seen lovers love in angst
Of awaiting moments
Not destined to sing a song.
Graceless beauty
Of a room has secrets to hold
For misery drops on us
Like the water
Flying from a nearby stream.
Let's play the notes then,
Lover, of endless tears
Yet endless belonging,
For it's not just in our hearts,
But etched to aching souls.

21. Gently Downstream

Feeling a gentle nudge
To share beyond wild daisies
Overgrowing on my head,
Holding memories of one kiss
Away from a monotonous crowd
Wearing vibrant ponchos.
One kiss turned to a hundred
In a sky that drew lines of fantasy
That I couldn't have dreamt of,
When you went downstream
And gently, oh so gently,
The bodies giggled with a sigh.
Hold back no more
Of sworn desires
Meant to be,
When we ride on paperboats
To the orgasmic skies.
Gentle touches of your skin,
Gentle biting on mine,
Hold what has to disguise
In fireflies over a winter canyon.
Wander, all over the terrain
Of my body, and be free and lost,

For I will guide you back if you need to,
Gently.
Gently, I will come,
And again,
For you and for our longing
Set upon a soul-stone
That we threw towards the river
Making it infinitely wild
Like you make me, gently stroking
My spots of warm senses.
Don't you say,
What love might not look like,
For you know,
What it looks like now,
And how gently this passion
Flows down,
While you swim downstream.

22. You Say You Love Me

You say you love me
And this is a moment of resonance
With cottages built by the hillside fog
And a bonfire in the open,
Where we maybe kissed
In eternal symphony.
It was a tug at my heart
That you sought to clear
From the traumas
Of autumn leaves
And summertime saga
That haunted my mind off myself
Before I found a piece of my soul
Etched to yours.
We talk about twin flames
Like they aren't a reality
In this carved world,
A facade we carry;
I longed for a pair of wild birds
That you finally showed me
Atop a cloud that floated
Like mayonnaise on my sandwich-top.
We danced a silly dance

Which you call stupid,
And I like it so,
Because I like you so.
With you beside me,
It feels like a brook breaking free
In its form of many
Amongst wildflowers
When you made love to me.

23. Traces

Traces.
More traces.
I imagine a porcupine
Setting the woods on fire.
I imagine neon pink shoes
Slowing down the pace of running cars.
I believe traces are left everywhere.
Of ashes and car-trails.
Screaming bats.
Screeching cars.
Traces of lost lives
And traces of lost lovers.
Do lost souls exist?
Your fingertips swallowed
My flesh whole
While they traced the tattoo
You made across the nape of my neck
Crookedly sitting atop my shoulders.
Traces of ink merged with my cells.
More traces.
You cuddle up with me
And breathe out on my cold neck.
More traces.

I am in love
With the signs
You leave me to pick.
I loved how you shouted
"I love you" that foggy evening
Breezy in the hills
For the wind to carry the traces.
Halting winds.
Moving hills.
I trace my way back to you.

24. Hillside Souls

We have escaped
The nullification of this world
For some eddying days,
By the ringing pines
And kissing lips.
When you took my hand
And led me away
To a place I had seen before
But never so,
Was the moment I felt bliss
Set in wet rocks in the hillside.
We wandered around a fire
Of warming hearts,
With feelings flying
In shattered doors
And cracking windows.
Don't go away from here,
So we could build a life
Of dirt and velvety cushions,
With whitewashed walls
To have our barefeet imprints
As hillside souls.

25. Finally

Here and now
We will all be gone away
Near, far wherever dust is blown away
And wildflowers bloom from the stones;
In this stone cold world
Where we don't belong.
We will flow through rivers
And we will run across them;
I'll feel my world in you,
I will speak my heart out to you,
I'll keep it warm on the cold nights
With warmth that I feel from you.
Our soul ignite tonight
Together, with fierce liberation;
You touch my demons free
And cast a fire over the lighthouse.
Your eyes are the only mirror I need—
They set me free,
I set you free,
I set us free, my Love.

Printed by Libri Plureos GmbH in Hamburg,
Germany